2.2

D1564123

IN LOVE AND SONG

DELIVERANCE
FROM THE EVERYDAY

As the astronauts observed, from their base on the moon, the first earth-rise ever witnessed by Man, they were strangely moved. Their reactions, however inarticulate, illustrate beautifully the poetic principle at work, and its method. How many men have been quickened into poetry at the sight of moon-rise here on earth, earth that has become commonplace and everyday through long familiarity! But now, for the astronauts, the confrontation was reversed. By the blast-off, an act of violence, consciousness had been catapulted into a new perspective. There on the horizon dawned their homeland planet, the too familiar earth: its beauty, its mystery, its pathos—the full meaning of that luminous and now remote sphere—was suddenly revealed. What the space-rocket did for the astronauts the poem can do for you and me. Contemplation of the too familiar from an unfamiliar viewpoint enables us to experience it once more.

By dealing with things, by making use of them, by becoming accustomed to them, as we say, we lose sight of them. Most of us pass through life in a state of semi-anaesthesia. The world about us has become so familiar that we are hardly aware of it. It is not sufficient that things be apprehended or the idea of them intellectually conveyed. If we are to re-experience them, they must be revealed anew. Poetry is revelation.

The revelation a poem offers us is a re-awakened awareness, a fresh re-experience of the world in all its sensory and emotional impact. We are not ordinarily in the mood to have such an awareness revived in us. There exists in all men a deep, instinctive, natural resistance to poetry. This resistance may show itself in one of several ways: indifference, embarrassment, ridicule, or active contempt. Marianne Moore indicates that she sympathizes with the last of these when she says, in her poem entitled "Poetry," "I, too, dislike it: there are things that are important beyond all this fiddle." And Nietzsche, himself a poet in the larger sense of the word, registers that same natural resistance in the form of combined ridicule and contempt when he is moved to cry out, "The poets? The poets lie too much." Plato, who declared that poets would be banished altogether from his ideal republic, might, perhaps, have agreed with him. And how many a grown man or woman has experienced, in the presence of poetry, sensations ranging from a mild embarrassment to an acute distaste!

Over our potential responses, our deeply buried emotions, a normal resistance stands guard. A native wariness, an instinctive reserve, bulwark us against the onslaughts of the poet. But these defenses are like the sonic barrier: the poet whose energy and craft enable him to break through them will meet with no further obstruction. Renewed awareness, the re-experience of carefully forgotten reality, that a poem awakens is, after all, once it has been achieved for us, a great good. A heightening and widening of consciousness then takes place, affording insights and exaltations that do not persist and that cannot, perhaps, even be recalled, during the lower, more comfortable moments of life. Aldous Huxley wrote of one of his characters that he believed in God, but only while the violins were playing, and who is there that hasn't felt an almost physical let-down on leaving the concert hall and finding himself once more in the noisy city street.

He has been breathing another air and is now "rejected into the world again." The point is that, as animals, we are anchored to this world by innumerable necessities, and our mistrust of that other realm of intensified feeling, insight and realization, which, at best, we can inhabit only momentarily, is instinctive and even, perhaps, necessary. Habit, routine, our daily humdrum apathy and indifference, this is the shield with which we protect ourselves from life while we are engaged in the business of living. It is the function of the arts to pierce that shield, to re-awaken in us a forgotten knowledge.

The strategies whereby the poet is enabled to outwit our natural resistance to poetry are many and various. We shall not catalogue them here. They are directed towards arousing us from an inborn, self-protective apathy, towards lulling our active aversion to anything that tries to shock us out of the sleep of habit, the sleep of daily living, into a painful, if exalted, realization of the act of living and of life itself. Our natural, and probably wholesome, apathy is a deep and stubborn thing. This normal, self-protective indifference is not easily overcome. To try to overwhelm us by frontal attack, by putting things down "in so many words," as we say, will not do it. If we are to have our eyes opened, if we are to be forced into renewed experience, we shall have to be tricked and startled out of our apathy. The trope or metaphor, the simplest and commonest device in the arsenal of poetry, does just this. By discovering hidden likenesses or analogies in things seemingly unlike, the poem surprises us, wrenches us, if you will, into renewed awareness of them.

All words are, of course, symbols. Many of them, and particularly compound words, originally were metaphors. But they have become worn with use. Fresh metaphors, compounded of a number of words in new relationships, are needed. The word *whitecaps,* for instance, denoting the foam scuffed up by wind in its passage over water, has lost, because of familiarity, its original metaphoric force, but when Swinburne describes whitecaps as ". . . where the wind's feet shine along the sea," they are not merely identified, they are experienced once more. Sometimes a metaphor or simile will occur in the midst of a poem so casually and unobtrusively as to seem almost accidental, and yet it will instantly cause everything that has gone before, or that comes after it, to fall into place. The reality rediscovered by the poem is, in that instant, by that metaphor or simile, as blindingly revealed as a darkened landscape by a flash of lightning. No amount of description or direct statement could so completely have done this. Such lines or phrases as "Time is a harper who plays until you fall asleep," "Among the guests star-scattered on the grass," ". . . not even the rain has such small hands," ". . . hung like those top jewels of the night," achieve immediacy by use of the same device.

A poem is what happens when a poet rediscovers, for himself, the reality we have lost sight of because, to use Shelley's metaphor, it has been overlaid by the veil of familiarity. The process, however, is not one of rediscovery and subsequent transmittal in a poem. The poem itself is part of the rediscovery. In making it, the poet learns what it is that he has rediscovered. Thus a child, when he begins to speak, learns what it is that he knows. And as a child will talk to himself, with no one around to hear, so in the poem the poet, it might be said, is talking to himself. He has established communication with his own being and therefore potentially with others. What was subject has become object. What was on the inside is now on the outside. It can be looked at and shared. The fact that, through language, this sharing can take place is proof of the identity of men, of their correspondences. Man is one Self. Those "others" are you.

J.H.W.

N.Y. February 1971

CONTENTS

IN LOVE AND SONG

I

Where are you hid from me, belovèd one
That I am seeking through the lonely world—
A wanderer, on my way home to you?

Where are you hid from me, belovèd one
That I am seeking through the lonely world—
A wanderer, on my way home to you?
Dark is the night, and perilous the road;
At many a breast in longing have I leaned,
At many a wayside worshipped—and my heart
Is tired from long travelling. Perhaps
In centuries to come you wait for me,
And are, as yet, an iris by the stream,
Lifting her single blossom, or the soft
Tremulous haze upon the hills—and we
Have missed each other. Oh, if it be so,
Then may this song reach to the verge of doom,
Ages unborn—to find you where you are,
My lonely one—and like a murmuring string,
Faint with one music, endlessly repeat,
To you not even knowing I was yours,
Her plaintive burden from the dolorous past
Of dusty legend, her archaic woe—
Telling of one upon a hopeless quest,
How, in the dark of time, he lost his way.

Lift your arms to the stars

Lift your arms to the stars
And give an immortal shout!
Not all the wells of darkness
Can put your beauty out.

You are armed with love, with love,
Nor all the powers of fate
Avail to do you harm—
Nor all the hands of hate.

What of good and evil,
Hell, and Heaven above—
Trample them with love!
Ride over them with love!

I roamed, in the gray evening, over field and hill—

I roamed, in the gray evening, over field and hill—
Above me the pale clouds were restless wanderers;
And when the day was gone and all the fields were still,
The thought of you was like a thousand stars.

Life burns us up like fire,

Life burns us up like fire,
And song goes up in flame;
The body returns in ashes
To the ashes whence it came.

Out of things it rises,
And laughs, and loves, and sings;
Slowly it subsides
Into the char of things.

Yet a voice soars above it—
Love is great and strong:
The best of us forever
Escapes, in love and song.

Toward the girl the boy's face turning
Kindles, with live eyes alert,
For he longs to wreak upon her
Loveliness the lovely hurt.

And she reads the wordless challenge,
And how swiftly she replies,
Darting scorn, in lightning challenge,
From the fury of her eyes.

Each in each, through veils of terror,
Recognizes, dimly known
Through dim powers, the dear power
That makes war upon its own.

Yet she has the woman's pity
For her lover, she arrays
For his joy her body's beauty,
Secretly, in many ways.

And to bathe amid the aura
Of her being, draw more near
To her maidhood, is his longing—
Dewy-fresh and morning-clear;

To avenge upon her beauty
All his ardor, to destroy
On her love the clear and crystal
Radiance of his running joy.

Till they merge, and flow together,
Intermingle, merge, and blend,
Weaving into one another
With hushed rapture, in the end.

Till the light yoke of her beauty
Chasten and subdue the stress
Of his wild and veering ardor,
Humbled in her loveliness.

In the evening, in the quiet Park, we walked together,
After so many and after so many years—
We walked again in the evening, in the warm May weather,
After the partings and tears.

And under the splendor, under the starry skies,
We walked, without sound or sigh, in a calm unbroken,
As the dead walk together in a long-lost Paradise—
Silent, with no word spoken.

My love is young and cruel,
Her lips cried laughingly,
"Come out to the old duel,
Cross swords, cross swords, with me.

"No quarter shall be given,
No mercy shall be shown;
Under the arch of heaven
Stand, or be overthrown."

Under the arch of heaven,
At the appointed place,
The awaited word was given,
And we stood face to face.

O dear, dark eyes and splendid!
Sweet lips that laughed apart!
Before the day was ended
The sword was in my heart.

Last evening, when the dew-drenched veil
Of mist and moonlight, phantom-pale,
All silver-soft and silent lay
Across the country far away,
Again I seemed to see you come,
As one at twilight turning home,
Over the glimmering moonlit fields
And meadows that the lowland yields.

In the far hollows soft asleep,
The mists like flocks of trooping sheep
Cloudily drifted here and there,
And a low murmur on the air,
Of crickets' and çicadas' sound,
Cradled the meadows miles around—
A dim susurrus, half-aloud.
Nearer you drifted like a cloud.

Some benediction of the blessed,
Some hovering pity, seemed to rest
On the mild country sorrow-stilled.
Across the night your presence thrilled,
That haunting aura drawing near;
My spirit trembled as in fear
Or joy, through all that lovely dread
Sensing, along the twilight shed,
Your onward being, dark and sweet—
The lingering slowness of your feet.

Doubtful I leaned, in drowsy mood—
When, suddenly, before me stood
Your breathing beauty, drenched with dew
Of dusk, and fragrant through and through
With breath of the wild country ways:
Veiled round in mist and shimmering haze
Of gauzy twilight starry-clear,
That tangible loveliness so near,
That vehement weight and sweet excess
Of your own very loveliness,
Almost I thought to reach and touch—
Nor dared, for longing overmuch.

The vague light of the moon, that shone
Cloud-covered, dimmed—and you were gone.

Beyond the dark, wide sea lie the enchanted isles,
Beyond the long horizon a music calls to me;
I see it in the sadness and smiling of your eyes,
I hear it in the far-off rustling of the sea.

O fair lands, lost at birth, that we shall never find!
O glad life passing by, and things that cannot be!
I see it in the sadness and smiling of your eyes,
I hear it in the far-off rustling of the sea.

I dreamed I passed a doorway
Where, for a sign of death,
White ribbons one was binding
About a flowery wreath.

What drew me so, I know not,
But drawing near, I said,
"Kind sir, and can you tell me
Who is it here lies dead?"

Said he, "Your most belovèd
Died here this very day,
That had known twenty Aprils,
Had she but lived till May."

Astonished, I made answer,
"Good sir, how say you so!
Here have I no belovèd,
This house I do not know."

Said he, "Who from forever
Was destined so to be
Here lies, your true belovèd,
Whom you shall never see."

I dreamed I passed a doorway
Where, for a sign of death,
White ribbons one was binding
About a flowery wreath.

Glimmering meadows, miles around,
Drenched with dew and drowsy sound,
Drink the moonlight and the dream;
Veiled in mists the lowlands gleam—
Through wild ways and fragrant aisles
Of the country, miles on miles,
Drifting cloudlike without will—
And soft mist is on the hill.

Everywhere earth's shrill delight
Shakes and shimmers through the night,
Silver tides of music flow
Round the world: the cricket's low
Harp, the starry ecstasy
Of the keen cicada's cry,
With "I love, I love, I love,"
To the cloudless moon above
Lift the old, the endless song;
And the firefly among
The low boughs and heavy leaves
His hushed flight in silence weaves—
Deeper than the love they sing,
The unutterable thing,
The sheer pang with which he glows,
Burns his body as he goes.

Now earth draws the trembling veil
From her bosom cloudy-pale,
And the bridegroom of the night
Flows to her in solemn light—
Memories of the absent sun
Dreaming of his lovely one.

From that fiery embrace
Wearied out, with lifted face,

Tangled hair, and dewy eyes,
Drowsed and murmurous she lies,
In the bride-sleep, the deep bliss
After some exalted kiss.

Fragrant is thy flowery hair,
O belovèd; everywhere,
Thy faint odor on the air,
From dread arches of thy grace
Wafted, what dark, secret place,
Curves of thy bright beauty, all
Lure me to wild love; the call
Of past lives is in my breast,
Intimations, dimly guessed,
Of seraphic, solemn things—
Mingled lips and murmurings,
On cool nights that gave me birth.
Yet, O mother, secret earth,
What stark mystery no less
Haunts the bosom that I press
Close against thy carelessness!

Where the tender poem of night,
In veiled music and moonlight,
Shimmering cries, and stars, and dreams,
Onward in soft rhythm streams—
With reluctant pulse and pause
To its timeless ending draws,
Mother, mother, yet I know
Of cool nights that whispered so
When I was not, long ago;
When thy beauty, murmuring low,
With abandon, like a bride,
Throws its glimmering veils aside,
This dread love I dare not say

Turns my trembling lips away—
Something deeper, something more
Than I ever guessed before,
A new homesickness at heart
Hungering for the home thou art:
As the rivers to the one
Sea with solemn longing run,
So my being to thy breast,
So my sorrow to thy rest.

Thou art mother, thou art bride,
By what dearer name beside
Must I name thee, must I call,
Who art dearer far than all?

On thy heart I lay my head—
Oh, what is it thou hast said!
Secret, beautiful and dread;
Lovely moment drawing near;
Thought, most terrible and dear,
Darling thought, and fearful, of
The dear fury of thy love
Even now that draws me down,
My faint body, to thine own—
Near and nearer yet, till I
Tangled in thy being lie—
Close, and close, for sheer excess
Wearied out with loveliness—
All this separate self, this me,
Soothed into the self of thee,
Rendered up in ecstasy!

Almost now thou seem'st to steal
From my breast the self, I feel
How my being everywhere,

As in dream, upon the air
Widens round me, till I grow
All I look on, overflow—
And into the life adored
All my very life is poured,
Through warm portals of thy heart
Hastening onward where thou art,
Who art all things: in the breeze
Stirring all the ruffled trees
To fresh whispers, how I pass
Upward through each blade of grass,
Tremble in moonlight, and rise
Looking out of other eyes—
Mystery of mysteries!
Pang of self, and tragical
Birth into the enlightened All!

Oh, dark rapture—to flow, press,
Cease, into thy loveliness,
With exalted weariness
Render up myself, and be,
Selfless, the dear self of thee—
In divine oblivion,
One with the belovèd one!

Where I press my burning face
Weeds and grasses interlace—
Sweetheart, are these dewy, soft
Tears for me, who must so oft
Perish of thee to be thine?
Deep I drink of you, divine
Elixir, bewildering wine.

In the grass my head is bowed,
The vague moon is in a cloud—

Ah, I cannot understand,
But the wind is like a hand
On my forehead, in caress,
And the earth is tenderness,
While around her sleeplessly
Shrills the restless will-to-be—
Lust for immortality
Shakes in sound, and floats in light,
Through the darkness: through the night
Clouds, and dreams, and fireflies,
And my songs of her arise.

There is a panther caged within my breast,
But what his name, there is no breast shall know
Save mine, nor what it is that drives him so,
Backward and forward, in relentless quest—
That silent rage, baffled but unsuppressed,
The soft pad of the stealthy feet that go
Over my body's prison to and fro,
Trying the walls forever without rest.

All day I feed him with my living heart,
But when the night puts forth her dreams and stars,
The inexorable frenzy reawakes:
His wrath is hurled upon the trembling bars,
The eternal passion stretches me apart,
And I lie silent—but my body shakes.

At night, in the old house of life I lie alone:
Spiders have fastened their soft webs, like clouds, between
Rafter and ceiling; threshold and gray floor are grown
Heavy with dust, where for so long no foot has been.

Mice, in the dark of the old walls, gnaw at the deep
Roots of the night, and softly on the dewy air
The cricket's song comes drifting in—even in sleep
I hear it, but I am too sorrowful to care.

He sings for unimaginable joy; he makes
Music, all night, of my lost youth; his happy cry
Thrills through the dark like a familiar voice, that wakes
In my unanswering breast hardly a memory.

Love has left me, and song has left me, and I know
I am a harp, silent to all those lovely things
That laid such hands upon me here so long ago.
Night deepens—echo slumbers along the strings.

So many a night with all its stars has come and gone,
Watching my rest; so many an evening all in vain
Has lit for me her trembling lamps. Sleep is upon
These eyelids, that are sealed in slumber and disdain.

Only the murmur, vaguely felt, of the hushed blood,
That on the shores of the old dream, like a vast sea,
Moves, in the darkness, mourning; and in the solitude
Of my heart's forest a far horn sounds drowsily.

I heard the owlet call,
A little, quavering call—
Timidly, timidly, out of the dark it cried:
It was midnight,
By candle-light
I sat alone, the light was burning low,
And I thought of you that once had loved me so,
And of my lonely youth, my stubborn pride.
Heart of my heart, it was you, out there in the night—
It was you that cried.

We lay by the sea, and knew
Darkness must make us one—
Heaven was thrilled clean through
By the trumpets of the sun,
The sea burned gold and blue.

The sand, in the pale heat,
Was parched as desert sand—
Your wrist, where the veins meet,
The cool veins of your hand,
Made thirst seem bitter-sweet.

Never a word was said
Of what must be so soon,
In longing and in dread
The golden afternoon
Burned down, till dusk was shed.

It was not hope, nor fear,
Yet something of them both,
That held us trembling here,
Half eager and half loath
For darkness, dread but dear.

Few were the words were spoken,
But in each other's eyes
We read the certain token
That sealed our destinies—
Our wings of pride were broken.

So, while the waters paled
Around us, and the west
Fainted, our hearts that failed,
In silence were confessed—
Silence at last prevailed.

And now up her clear stair
The evening-star began
To climb, where heaven was bare
A homing fish-hawk ran
Down avenues of air.

Night swallowed up the sun,
And darkness, like a hood,
Sank, and the sea breathed on—
In silence and solitude
Love's very will was done.

As the still moon without stir
Draws the waters after her,
The sad robe of all the sea,
Silently thou drawest me.

As the billows on the shore,
To be broken and give o'er,
Dash themselves in dying spray,
So I perish, even as they.

Lethe soft, ah, sweet surcease—
Not the wave may be at peace
Till it shatter, nor love rest
Save at the belovèd breast.

My sister, my spouse, is as a secret spring,
A fountain of light under the brows of the morn,
A garden of quiet rest;
Under her side the melancholy sorrowing
Of ancient sadness is, and under her breast
The joy of the unborn.

My flower, my love, is as a shining star,
As a young rose hid in the windy grass,
A song in the land of death—
The mournful beauty of all brief things that are,
A passionate and unavailing breath,
A soft "alas."

My sister, my dove, is as a bundle of myrrh,
A house of delights, a garden of pleasant length,
A shady and pleasant tree;
Her breast is the mansion of certain dreams that were,
And her pale breast a promise of things to be,
A sorrowful strength.

As a cool wood is my own, my sister, my dove,
A giver of life, a gate to the land of breath,
A stooping and shady cloud—
As a sad secret bared for the eyes of love,
A futile defiance, sorrowful and proud,
Of ancient death.

You came—and like a stormy wind your love
Blew over the lone waters, and the sea
Of my heart's life was shaken violently,
And all the trembling waves began to move,

And cried their love out to the shore, and cast
Their love upon the shore—but you were gone!
Yet still that restless flood is roaring on,
Where once so brief a storm in fury passed.

And still, from the calm heaven of my mind,
My thought, like a great hawk on lonely wing,
Watches those waters laboring, laboring,
In troubled multitude, broken and blind.

Room that I have loved, now are we come to parting,
I leave with you the dream lost beyond recall—
Softly through the window pours the lonely moonlight,
Slumbers on the bed, slumbers on the wall.

Faint in glimmering fields the grasshoppers are shrilling,
As on nights of old; and a cricket, too,
Sounds his tender note solemnly and slowly—
Leaves, in the hushed light, glisten, bright with dew.

Here is the low table where we laughed together,
Chairs, where we have sat, huddle side by side:
In the quiet night the darkened house is musing
Upon vanished days and old hopes that died.

Where my youth has sorrowed, now lies only moonlight,
Moonlight on the bed, moonlight on the floor—
And across the pillow where your head lay dreaming,
O my lost belovèd, moonlight evermore.

II

The world, with all her winds and waters, earth and air,
Fields, folds, and moving clouds.

On the large highway of the ample air that flows
Unbounded between sea and heaven, while twilight screened
The sorrowful distances, he moved and had repose;
On the huge wind of the immensity he leaned
His steady body, in long lapse of flight—and rose

Gradual, through broad gyres of ever-climbing rest,
Up the clear stair of the untrammelled sky, and stood
Throned on the summit! Slowly, with his widening breast,
Widened around him the enormous solitude,
From the gray rim of ocean to the glowing west.

Headlands and capes forlorn, of the far coast, the land
Rolling her barrens toward the west, he, from his throne
Upon the gigantic wind, beheld: he hung, he fanned
The abyss, for mighty joy, to feel beneath him strown
Pale pastures of the sea, with heaven on either hand—

The world, with all her winds and waters, earth and air,
Fields, folds, and moving clouds. The awful and adored
Arches and endless aisles of vacancy, the fair
Void of sheer heights and hollows, hailed him as her lord
And lover in the highest, to whom all heaven lay bare.

Till from that tower of ecstasy, that baffled height,
Stooping, he sank; and slowly on the world's wide way
Walked, with great wing on wing, the merciless, proud Might,
Hunting the huddled and lone reaches for his prey,
Down the dim shore—and faded in the crumbling light.

Slowly the dusk covered the land. Like a great hymn
The sound of moving winds and waters was; the sea
Whispered a benediction, and the west grew dim
Where evening lifted her clear candles quietly. . . .
Heaven, crowded with stars, trembled from rim to rim.

Grasshopper, your airy song
And my poem alike belong
To the dark and silent earth,
From which all poetry has birth;
All we say and all we sing
Is but as the murmuring
Of that drowsy heart of hers
When from her deep dream she stirs:
If we sorrow, or rejoice,
You and I are but her voice.

Deftly does the dust express,
In mind, her hidden loveliness—
And, from her cool silence, stream
The cricket's cry and Dante's dream;
For the earth, that breeds the trees,
Breeds cities too, and symphonies,
Equally her beauty flows
Into a savior, or a rose—
Looks down in dream, and from above
Smiles at herself in Jesus' love;
Christ's love and Homer's art
Are but the workings of her heart,
Through Leonardo's hand she seeks
Herself, and through Beethoven speaks
In holy thunderings that sound
The awful message of the ground.

The serene and humble mold
Does in herself all selves enfold,
Kingdoms, destinies, and creeds,
Proud dreams, heroic deeds,
Science, that probes the firmament,
The high, inflexible intent
Of one, for many, sacrificed;

Plato's brain, the heart of Christ,
All love, all legend, and all lore
Are in the dust forevermore.

Even as the growing grass,
Up from the soil religions pass,
And the field that bears the rye
Bears parables and prophecy—
Out of the earth the poem grows,
Like the lily, or the rose;
And all man is, or yet may be,
Is but herself in agony
Toiling up the steep ascent
Toward the complete accomplishment
When all dust shall be—the whole
Universe—one conscious soul.

Ah, the quiet and cool sod
Bears in her breast the dream of God.

If you would know what earth is, scan
The intricate, deep heart of man,
Which is the earth articulate,
And learn how holy and how great,
How limitless, and how profound,
Is the nature of the ground—
How, without question or demur,
We may entrust ourselves to her
When we are wearied out and lay
Our bodies in the common clay.

For she is pity, she is love,
All wisdom, she; all thoughts that move
About her everlasting breast
Till she gathers them to rest—

All tenderness of all the ages,
Seraphic secrets of the sages,
Vision and hope of all the seers,
All prayer, all anguish, and all tears,
Are but the dust, that from her dream
Awakes, and knows herself supreme;
Are but earth, when she reveals
All that her secret heart conceals
Down in the dark and silent loam,
Which is ourselves, asleep, at home.

Yes, and this, my poem, too,
Is part of her as dust and dew—
Wherein herself she doth declare,
Through my lips, and say her prayer.

Morning draws near. Already watery gleams
Seep through, diluting darkness; premonitions
Of dawn run on the air; imminent light
Wells fire along the horizon. Day is waking!
By shore and dune, in meadow, marsh and wood,
To the old torment, to the bloody task
And tragedy of being, to the delight,
The longing and the wonder, life is waking!
Faint pipings prick the dusk, preludes to joy
At the coming of the god; the robin first
With frenzied caroling gives thanks; the wren,
The oriole, chewink, flicker and chat
Sound jubilant assent; the thrushes last
With solemn chant antiphonal proclaim
Resurrection and return. Spirit is waking!
The spirit that sleeps in metal and in stone,
In flower and tree, in water, earth and air,
And in the spinning demons of the atom,
And in the stars, and in the beast in man,
Sleeps, but is growing restless and shall win
A way out of its prison. Hope is waking!
All time present and all time to come,
All time past—the past, which has been the future,
As the future shall be the past—all spirits living,
All spirits that were, all spirits yet to be,
In this brief moment, this eternal now,
Wait on that hope: we are all here together.

The broad beach,
Sea-wind and the sea's irregular rhythm,
Great dunes with their pale grass, and on the beach
Driftwood, tangle of bones, an occasional shell,
Now coarse, now carven and delicate—whorls of time
Stranded in space, deaf ears listening
To lost time, old oceanic secrets.
Along the water's edge, in pattern casual
As the pattern of the stars, the pin-point air-holes,
Left by the sand-flea under the receding spume,
Wink and blink out again. A gull drifts over,
Wide wings crucified against the sky—
His shadow travels the shore, upon its margins
You will find his signature: one long line,
Two shorter lines curving out from it, a nearly
Perfect graph of the bird himself in flight.
His footprint is his image fallen from heaven.

Nec mea qui digitis lumina condat erit

The gnu up at the Zoo
Has closed his eyes in death,
He was a very patient gnu
Who never made too much to-do
Until he was out of breath.
Few there were understood him,
Very few understood him—
Now he is gone
I mourn alone
That most untimely death.

The ape who had no shape
Went over the hill today,
He always wanted to escape
Until he discovered a way—
And he closed his eyes
In sheer surprise
When he found he was dead, they say.
Many there are will mourn him,
Many who once did scorn him,
And some there are will pray.

I pray every day
For all things that draw breath—
For the ape and the gnu
Up at the Zoo,
For the turtle-dove and the tiger too,
I pray with every breath.
But chiefly for myself I pray,
And for the staring fish that may
Not close their eyes by night or day—
No, not even in death.

(*For Van Wyck Brooks*)

Look, on the topmost branches of the world
The blossoms of the myriad stars are thick;
Over the huddled rows of stone and brick
A few sad wisps of empty smoke are curled,
Like ghosts languid and sick.

One breathless moment now the city's moaning
Fades, and the endless streets seem vague and dim.
There is no sound around the whole world's rim,
Save in the distance a small band is droning
Some desolate old hymn.

Van Wyck, how often have we been together
When this same moment made all mysteries clear:
The infinite stars that brood above us here,
And the gray city in the soft June weather,
So tawdry and so dear.

Heaven is full of stars to-night, the earth
Lies hushed, as she shall lie some day perhaps,
When life and death no longer trouble her—
No voice, no cry, in the whole countryside.
The empty road rambles through field and thicket,
And in the road are prints of hoof and foot:
Along the surface of this lonely planet,
Now naked to the hunger of the stars,
Man and beast—on the old pilgrimage—
They passed together here, not long ago.

What was it they were looking for, I wonder,
Or if, themselves, they knew? Where were they going?
Footsteps—always footsteps going somewhere—
What country is it that they all are seeking,
Who up and down the world, by night or day,
Move with such patience, always to one end?

Not the least sound. Not the least leaf disturbs
The immemorial reticence of heaven.
Footprints—only footprints going somewhere. . . .

Wherever they were going, they are gone.

The fish-hawk over the water and the pale fish that goes
Glimmering through the water—the preyer and the prey—
They follow or hasten ever; they wrestle together, they close
In the old fearful fashion, in the old fierce way.

Harsh are the rites of being, and bitter is the war
Waged between life and life by the blind will-to-be—
Yet all, if they but knew it, are one: lovers they are,
Who strive, each with the other, in a great mystery.

All afternoon, drowsing here, I have heard,
In the west wood nearby,
A vireo's quick, reiterate, questioning call,
Like water, dripping, fall
Into the silence. No least wind has stirred,
Even with the softest sigh,
The little leaves to turn the other cheek,
Rough side or sleek.
Light is stiff in bush and tree,
Great light is over all.
Now there will be,
Deep in the tunnelled shade
And on the winding walks mossy with time,
Siftings of light on darkness laid.
The vireo's call measures the afternoon—
And high in the western heaven, see!
Clear as a chime,
The snow-pale moon.

Already it's late summer. Sun-bathers go
Earlier now. Except for those who lie
Dazed between sea-music and radio
The beach is bare as the blue bowl of the sky,
Where a cloud floats, solitary and slow.

And up the beach, where at mid-summer's height
One gull with occasional lurch and pause would steer
Onward his leisurely loose-winged casual flight,
Gull wings weave patterns, their noise floods the ear
Like a fugue, cry answering cry in hoarse delight.

Now on the beach there also may be found,
Straddled in mimic flight, with arching wing
Spread either way, some gull swift death has downed
There, like a tumbled kite whose severed string
Kept it in heaven by binding it to the ground.

Inland, when the slant evening sun-beams touch
Leaves, long obscured in tunnelled shade, to flame,
The divine insect, for I called him such,
Begins his high thin music. To my shame
I never learned what he was, who owe him so much.

Listening to his frail song, so pure, so dim,
I made my poems, he was mystery's decoy,
Something far and lost, just over the rim
Of being, or so I felt, and as a boy
I wove fantastic notions about him.

Throughout long evenings and hushed midnights when
Grasshoppers shrilled, his barely perceptible note
Wound on like a thread of time, while my pen
Made its own scratchy music as I wrote.
The divine insect and I were comrades then.

That high hypnotic note opened some door
On a world seemingly come upon by chance,
But a world, surely, I had known before.
Deeper I sank into a timeless trance—
Strange thoughts and fancies troubled me more and more.

I could pass through that minuscule sound, it seemed to me,
As through a fine tube, getting smaller and still more small,
Until I was smaller than nothing—then, suddenly,
Come to the other end of the tube, and crawl
Out, into glittering immensity.

For, if by travelling west you shall come east
Or, as Einstein has it, the continuum
Curves on itself, may we not through the least
Come to the largest, and so finally come
Back where we were, undiminished and unincreased?

Since then, I have tried to put this into verse,
But language limits the sense it often mars—
I still believe, for better or for worse,
We look through one atom into all the stars,
In the note of one insect hear the universe.

These few green acres where so many a day
Has found me, acres I have loved so long,
Have the whole galaxy for crown, and stay
Unspoiled by that. Here in some thrush's song
I have heard things that took my breath away.

It is a country out of the world's ken,
Time has no power upon it. Year on year,
Summer unfolds her pageant here again—
I have looked deep into all being here
Through one loved place far from the storms of men.

Here often, day and night, there will be heard
The sea's grave rhythm, a dark undertone
Beneath the song of insect or of bird—
Sea-voices by sea-breezes landward blown,
And shudder of leaves by the soft sea-wind stirred.

In the jade light and gloom of woodland walks
The spider lily and slender shinleaf stand,
The catbird from his treetop pulpit talks
The morning up, and in the meadowland
The velvet mullein lift their woolly stalks.

The world grows old. Ageless and undefiled
These stay, meadow and thicket, wood and hill:
The green fly wears her golden dress, the wild
Grape is in bloom, the fork-tailed swallow still
Veers on the wind as when I was a child.

And in mid-August, when the sun has set
And the first star out of the west shows through,
The divine insect, as I call him yet,
Begins his high thin note, so pure, so true,
Putting me ever deeper in his debt.

The old enchantment takes me as before,
I listen, half in dream, hearing by chance
The soft lapse of the sea along the shore,
And sink again into that timeless trance,
Deeper and deeper now, and more and more.

To get off the ground has always been difficult
For poet or bird, and the gray gull
At the sea's edge here, who regards me with an eye
That is sceptical, shall we say, would never try
To scale heaven by direct assault—
Ascent is always oblique and casual.

But the wings must be kept ready. He stretches his wings
To keep them ready; those huge vans,
Feathered, curving forefingers, reach upward again,
Arch outward, are shaken, are slowly lowered; and then,
With curious rufflings and fidgetings,
Fold back onto the body like collapsed fans.

The sea's blue crescent, the harsh smell of the sea,
Her thunders, this perpetual roar,
These vacant beaches, are background for a bird
With whom I have always wanted to have a word—
Theories of flight interest me.
I advance upon him boldly along the shore

And begin: "O master of ascent"—
When, suddenly, the great wings on either side
Canopy out; with lumbering gait he runs
Into the wind; then, all at once
(So imperceptible was the event),
Is mounted upon the wind his wings bestride.

He climbs seaward, leaving me breathless here.
Now, as he travels, gaining height,
Those two webbed feet, symbolic of his birth,
His bondage to sea and earth,
Are quietly retracted, landing gear
Needed for the interval between flight and flight.

When I went forth in the morning with all my gear,
In battle array, with proud banner flying,
The great mother who had sent me forth was there
To cheer me on. Her peepers in the marsh were crying
And it was the spring of the year.

When I came home in the evening, in darkness drear
And sorry array, with no proud banner flying,
The great mother who had sent me forth was there
To take me back. Now I am lying
At her heart in the spring of the year.

Earth and the ancient joy are ever young—
When has she changed, for all her many days!
The cloudy banners of her hope are hung,
Spring after spring, through all the woodland ways.

The meditations of the secret earth
Are steadfast and enduring—these remain:
Her sacramental rites of death and birth,
And the old mysteries of love and pain.

Time and the years like wandering clouds go by:
The moon still floods the wood, and from the hill
The cricket lifts the immemorial cry—
And the immortal joy is flowing still.

Du bist Orplid, mein Land, das ferne leuchtet—MÖRIKE

I

This is enchanted country, lies under a spell,
Bird-haunted, ocean-haunted—land of youth,
Land of first love, land of death also, perhaps,
And desired return. Sea-tang and honeysuckle
Perfume the air, where the old house looks out
Across mild lowlands, meadows of scrub and pine,
A shell echoing the sea's monotone
That haunts these shores. And here, all summer through,
From dawn to dusk, there will be other music,
Threading the sea's music: at rise of sun,
With jubilation half-awakened birds
Salute his coming again, the lord of life,
His ambulatory footstep over the earth,
Who draws after him all that tide of song—
Salute the oncoming day, while from the edges
Of darkness, westward, fading voices call,
Night's superseded voices, the whip-poor-will's
Lamentation and farewell. Morning and noon
And afternoon and evening, the singing of birds
Lies on this country like an incantation:
Robin and wren, catbird, phoebe and chat,
Song-sparrow's music-box tune, and from the slender
Arches of inmost shade, the woodland's roof,
Where few winds come, flutelike adagio or
Wild syrinx-cry and high raving of the thrush,
Their clang and piercing pierce the spirit through—
Look off into blue heaven, you shall witness
Angelic motions, the volt and sidewise shift
Of the swallow in mid-air. Enchanted land,
Where time has died; old ocean-haunted land;
Land of first love, where grape and honeysuckle

Tangle their vines, where the beach-plum in spring
Snows all the inland dunes; bird-haunted land,
Where youth still dwells forever, your long day
Draws to its close, bringing for evening-star
Venus, a bud of fire in the pale west,
Bringing dusk and the whip-poor-will again,
And the owl's tremolo and the firefly,
And gradual darkness. Silently the bat,
Over still lawns that listen to the sea,
Weaves the preoccupation of his flight.
The arch of heaven soars upward with all its stars.

II

Summer fades soon here, autumn in this country
Comes early and exalted. Where the wild land,
With its sparse bayberry and huckleberry,
Slopes seaward, where the seaward dunes go down,
Echoing, to the sea; over the beaches,
Over the shore-line stretching east and west,
The ineffable slant light of autumn lingers.
The roof of heaven is higher now, the clouds
That drag, trailing, along the enormous vault,
Hang higher, the wide ways are wider now.
Sea-hawks wander the ocean solitudes,
Sea-winds walk there, the waters grow turbulent,
And inland also a new restlessness
Walks the world, remembering something lost,
Seeking something remembered: wheeling wings
And songless woods herald the great departure,
Cattle stray, swallows gather in flocks,
The cloud-travelling moon through gusty cloud
Looks down on the first pilgrims going over,
And hungers in the blood are whispering, "Flee!
Seek otherwhere, here is no lasting home."

Now bird-song fails us, now an older music
Is vibrant in the land—the drowsy cry
Of grasshopper and cricket, earth's low cry
Of sleepy love, her inarticulate cry,
Calling life downward, promising release
From these vague longings, these immortal torments.
The drowsy voice drones on—oh, siren voice:
Aeons of night, millenniums of repose,
Soundless oblivion, divine surcease,
Dark intermingling with the primal darkness,
Oh, not to be, to slough this separate being,
Flow home at last! The alert spirit listens,
Hearing, meanwhile, far off, along the coast,
Rumors of the rhythm of some wakeful thing,
Reverberations, oceanic tremors,
The multitudinous motions of the sea,
With all its waters, all its warring waves.

The ritual of dawn ended, the jubilant choirs
That hailed the divine return, the victory over night,
And those high lonely later voices
Heard toward morning at the edge of light,
Now folded into their peace, all passion spent,
He mounts the platform of the nearest tree
And begins, almost too clearly perhaps,
To explain everything—
His argument rips the heart out of mystery.

The first statement is certainly plain,
Possibly incontrovertible: "From this,"
So he says, "it follows—but, to go back again
To our premise—for instance, the word, *is*,
As meaning (considered, of course, ontologically
From the standpoint taken—the term is somewhat loose
In the context—); now, then, we—
To go back once more—from this deduce
The essential factors. Therefore, by inference, and—"

I am not certain that I understand,
But out of a cloud the sun looks down at me
And I am sitting here quite comfortably,
A meadow and a wood on either hand,
And am inclined to agree.

In the immense cathedral of the holy earth,
Whose arches are the heavens and the great vault above
Groined with its myriad stars, what miracles of birth,
What sacraments of death, what rituals of love!

Her nave is the wide world and the whole length of it,
One flame on all her altars kindles her many fires;
Wherever the clear tapers of trembling life are lit
Resound for joy the old, indomitable choirs.

The holy church of earth with clamorous worshippers
Is crowded, and fierce hungers, faithful every one
To the one faith; that stern and simple faith of hers
Contents the heart that asks no pity, giving none.

Each on the other feeds, and all on each are fed,
And each for all is offered—a living offering, where
In agony and triumph the ancient feast is spread,
Life's sacramental supper, that all her sons may share.

They mingle with one another, blend—mingle—merge, and
        flow
Body into wild body; in rapture endlessly
Weaving, with intricate motions of being, to and fro,
The pattern of all Being, one mighty harmony:

One Body, of all bodies woven and interwrought—
One Self, in many selves, through their communion
In love and death, made perfect, wherein each self is nought
Save as it serve the many, mysteriously made One.

And all are glad for life's sake, and all have found it good
From the beginning; all, through many and warring ways,
In savage vigor of life and wanton hardihood
Live out, like a brave song, the passion of their days.

With music woven of lust and music woven of pain,
Chapel and aisle and choir, the great cathedral rings—
One voice in all her voices chanting the old disdain
Of pity, the clean hunger of all primal things.

From the trembling of Arcturus even to the tiny nest
Of the grey mouse, the glories of her vast frame extend:
The span of her great arches, stretching from east to west,
Is measureless—the immense reaches are without end.

※　　※　　※

Evening closes. The light from heaven's west window falls
Graver and softer now. In vain the twilight pleads
With stubborn night—his shadow looms on the massive walls.
Darkness. The immemorial ritual proceeds.

The spider in her quivering web watches and waits;
The moth flutters entangled, in agony of fear
He beats among the toils that bind him; she hesitates
Along the trembling wires—she pauses—she draws near,

She weaves her delicate bondage around him; in the net,
As in a shroud, he labors—but, labor as he will,
The cunning threads hold fast; her drowsy mouth is set
Against the body that shivers softly, and is still.

And through the leafy dark the owl with noiseless flight
Moves, peering craftily among the tangled trees
And thickets of the wood all slumbrous in the night—
The fledgling's bitter cry comes sharp upon the breeze.

With dreadful ceremony all things together move
To the one end: shrill voices in triumph all around
Prolong deliriously their monotone of love—
Arches and aisles are heavy with incense and dim sound.

Hush, the whole world is kneeling! Murmurous is the air—
The Host is lifted up. Upon the altar lies
The sacramental Body. The wind breathes like a prayer—
Solemnly is renewed the eternal sacrifice.

With mingled moan and might of warring wills made one
The vast cathedral shudders. From chancel, nave and choir
Sounds the fierce hymn to life: her holy will be done!
Upon her myriad altars flames the one sacred fire.

Toward dawn I came awake hearing a crow,
Perched on the roof-tree, lift his guttural cry
Twice on the shaken air of morning. No
Caw, answering, made reply.
The wood shivered, a wind began to sigh
Among the boughs already growing bare,
As drowsily I waited—and once more
That raucous question shook the vacant air.
Silence settled back slowly, as before.
I turned to sleep; I heard, half-waking there,
His harsh, vehement caw lifted again.
The frosty dawn was silent on the hill,
Silence over the listening wood—and then,
Faintly, from far away,
The answer came. Morning flowed into day.
All was still.

Now there is silence. Among the voices of the coming spring
Yours will be silent. What shall be said of you, who lie
Propped here so still in your nest upon the swaying bough?
Out of nothing there came a need, a mouth, a cry,
Out of peace, a suffering,
Drawn back into it now.

Oh, that I might be again
In the leafy solitudes
Where the ancient beauty broods
And the heart is healed of pain!

In a certain hidden place
Shined on by the evening-star,
Where the woods and waters are
Dear as a belovèd face.

'Tis a country to my mind:
All the hills and heights are green,
With clear meadows in between—
All the woods and ways are kind.

There the spider all day long
Spins her web with cunning skill,
And the cricket on the hill
Makes one music of his song.

Night and day, a dreamy noise
Hovers round it—night and day;
And the world is far away,
And the silence has a voice.

In the lowlands, in the deep
Solitude for miles around,
To a hushed and happy sound
Time itself has fallen asleep.

Oh, that I were there again,
By the meadows drenched with dew!
Where the ancient dream comes true,
And the heart is healed of pain.

The work of wind and wave is never done,
The stars keep timeless vigil; this, our life,
Is to their high, austere fidelity
As is the idle jigging of a fife
To the great task and silence of the sun,
The termless roar and labor of the sea.

Stars have their glory and, or near or far,
Are worth our worship, as all glories are;
There is a star I worship, early and late—
The sun men call it, drinking from that great
Fountain of light, the glory of a star.

III

And I put on my bathing suit, the better one,
I like it better than the wetter one,

When the beach is tawny in the sun and the sky has only
Little feathery question-marks of cloud
And the sea dances, and I'm feeling far from lonely,
And a friend who thinks very loud and talks very loud
About Kierkegaard, Kafka, Rilke and Mallarmé,
Melville and James, in that peculiar way,
Night and day,
Invites me to take a little walk with him
Down the beach and have a little talk with him,
I always go, plodding along through the deep sand,
    because I know it's very good for me.

When the sea is wrinkled with cold and the wind is blowing,
And I got up late and am feeling rather dim
And decide to go back, and a friend says, "Where are you going?
The water's wonderful, come on in for a swim,"
I hurry to take off my clothes in the bathing-box:
Coat, pants, shirt, drawers, undershirt, shoes and socks
With the white clocks—
And I put on my bathing suit, the better one,
I like it better than the wetter one,
And I plunge in, without a moment's hesitation, because
    I realize it's extremely beneficial to my health.

When I'm sitting with a lovely girl, who is growing dearer
Every moment, she is so sweet, and a moon all gold
Looks into the garden, and she says, "Won't you come
    a little nearer?
It's draughty there—I'm afraid of your catching cold;"
And there's music perhaps, the twang of a lone guitar,
And a voice somewhere, singing, and one star
Not too far,
If I feel the least tickling in nose or throat
I go in and put on my overcoat,
Because I've been given to understand that these premoni-
    tory symptoms must on no account be neglected.

In nature's order, the grand hierarchy
Of snakes and poets, bankers, swallows, skunks,
There is an underlying unity
Embracing all, whatever they may be:
Bishops or archbishops,
Angels or archangels,
Monks or chipmunks.

There were footsteps on the stairway, uncertain
Sounds he had never heard, more like the flopping
Of a chicken than the tread of a man. The night
Tensed, and he waited. Yet soon
All was quiet, and he could relax—first, though,
Take a look-see. Nothing there. Then,
Perplexed but in bed once more,
Suddenly, in that moment when he was about
To fall asleep, he
Fell asleep.

After one more grandiloquent effort he slips back—
Slumping? Oh no, he may be down but he's never out
(Probably wishes he were); now, pondering a fresh attack,
He wheels his slender, simonized bulk about,

Fumbles at the slippery surface until he has come to grips,
Mounts, very slowly, with ever-increasing hope, and then
Mounts, more slowly, with ever-increasing hope—and slips
All the way down to the bottom of the tub again;

Lies there, motionless, pretty discouraged perhaps? not he—
It's dogged as does it, keep your chin up, don't take
No for an answer, etc.—he plots a new strategy,
The oblique approach. This, too, turns out to be a mistake.

The enamelled surface of his predicament
Resembles those pockets in time and space that hold
Sick minds in torture, his struggle is a long argument
With a fact that refuses to be persuaded or cajoled.

Midnight finds him still confident. I slink to bed,
Worn out with watching. The suave heavens turn
Blandly upon their axis, overhead
The constellations glitter their polite unconcern.

Toward morning, hounded by anxiety, slumberless,
I post to the scene. Where is he? The enamelled slopes below,
Vacant—the uplands, vacant—a bathtub full of emptiness,
The insoluble problem solved! But how? Something no
        one of us, perhaps, will ever know.

Unless he went down the drain?

(With apologies to the author of Macbeth, *whoever he may be.)*

A rabbit has very few things,
And it doesn't seem quite fair:
He has ears but he has no wings,
He has fur but he has no hair,
He enchants yet he seldom sings;
But he has a sleeve of care.
When he doffs it at dusk, sleep will tend it,
Is it just a little worn? sleep will mend it—
Sleep that knits up the rabbit's sleeve of care.

A rabbit will seldom roam
Yet you'll find him everywhere,
When he's out, then he's at home,
When he's home, he's out somewhere;
And he uses his brush for a comb,
To comb his sleeve of care.
When he dons it at dawn, sleep has tended it,
Was it just a little worn? sleep has mended it—
Sleep that knits up the rabbit's sleeve of care.

A rabbit needs little sleep
But he's got to have his share,
His thoughts are very deep
When he has the time to spare;
And he'll worry himself to sleep
Over his sleeve of care.
But a little sleep will make it new again,
A little sleep will make it do again—
Sleep that knits up the rabbit's sleeve of care.

A bird with a big eye
In at my open window poked his head,
And fixed me with a big eye.
"Who are you? What do you want?" I said.
"Me? You mean you don't know me?" he made reply,
"Why, I am I. Who are you?"
"I, too, am I," I bashfully admitted.
Now here was a big I-dea to work upon,
For if each one is I, must we not all be one?
Then I am one in all, and all are one in me.
I observed, thinking it over carefully,
That I wondered, this being true,
What made us feel so separate, so alone.
"*I* did," shouted the bird,
And I turned to strangle him, but he was flown.

"You mean to say," I said,
"I made up the universe out of my head?"

"Sure," he said.

"I'm amazed," I said.

"Go on! You know it's so.
I know you know."

"What you mean?" I said.

"I mean like I said.
You made up the universe out of your head,
And maintain it still
By an act of will."

"You sure that's true?"

"Sure. All that worrying you do
Keeps the grass green and the sky blue."

"Gosh," I said,
"What'll happen when I die?"

"You won't have time to know I was right—
The whole damn thing'll go out like a light."

"You mean that?" I said.

"Sure," he said.
"Why don't you try?
It's nice to try."

A hippopotamus had a bride
    Of rather singular beauty,
When he lay down at her side
    'Twas out of love, not duty—
    Hers was an exceptional beauty.
Take, oh take those lips away, etc.

He met her in Central Nigeria,
    While she was resident there,
Where life is distinctly superior
    And a hippo can take down her hair—
    And, God, but she was fair!
Take, oh take those lips away, etc.

She was coming up from her morning swim
    When first they chanced to meet:
He looked at her, she looked at him,
    And stood with reluctant feet
    Where mud and river meet.
Take, oh take those lips away, etc.

Their eye-beams, twisted on one thread,
    Instantaneously did twine,
And he made up poetry out of his head,
    Such as: "Dear heart, be mine"—
    And he quoted, line for line,
"Hail to thee, blithe spirit", etc.

Now, hippopotamoid courtesy
    Is strangely meticulous—
A beautiful thing, you will agree,
    In a hippopotamus—
    And she answered, briefly, thus:
"Hail to thee, blithe spirit", etc.

Perhaps she was practising the arts
    That grace old Hippo's daughter,
The coquetries that win all hearts,
    For, even as he besought her,
    She slid into the water.
Out, out, brief candle, etc.

Now, on the borders of the wood,
    Whence love had drawn him hither,
He paces in an anguished mood,
    Darting hither and thither
    In a terrific dither.
Out, out, brief candle, etc.

The course of true love never yet
    Ran smooth, so we are told,
With thorns its pathway is beset
    And perils manifold,
    So was it from of old.
Out, out, brief candle, etc.

Yet soon a happier morning smiles,
    The marriage feast is spread—
The flower girls were crocodiles,
    When hippopotamus led
    Hippopotamus, with firm tread,
    A bride to the bridal bed.
Milton, thou should'st be living at this hour.

Gulls, that live by the water and hang around docks,
Know about fish, how to fetch them out of the sea—
They know, also, how to split clams on rocks,
But nothing (and this gives them a certain dignity)
About "the seriousness of the present world situation."

The squirrel, that is so clever at cracking a nut
And indulges in such fascinating antics,
Can walk, head first, down the trunk of a tree, but
Knows little, if anything, about semantics—
The impression he leaves with me is rather a pleasant one.

There is an alligator lives in the Zoo,
Who is gifted, though he neither paints nor sings—
He has made an art of having nothing better to do,
Never gets nervous or "takes a grave view of things."
I find him, for some reason or other, extremely attractive.

Do you think the world will end with a bang or a whimper?
I'm rather inclined to think it won't end with a bang—
More probably with a simper,
Like that on the face of the little orang-outang
In Bronx Park, when he's feeling so pleased with himself.

It was annoying to be kept awake,
Last night, by a rodent working in the wall,
Yet this one was an artist and for art's sake,
Or so I am told, should be forgiven all.
His art was penetrating, and unique
In its grasp of the essential material;
After last night I will concede him to be,
For resonance, for sheer intensity,
Distinction of tone and firmness of technique,
The outstanding tooth of our time in all rodentry.

For the past two hours now
You have repeated the same note
Until I flinch at the mere thought of it.
Determination,
Functioning within discreet limits
To a well-defined end,
Is not ignoble,
But you have yet to learn when enough is enough.
Why labor the point
Of what already two hours ago
I had been willing to concede—
An assertion
In any case
Remarkable for nothing
Other than the pertinacity it so painfully exemplifies?
Now take yourself off
And let me hear no more about it;
Your note
Lacks the subtlety that would give its overtones
Implications worthy of the theme you essay.

EARTH

(With apologies to The New Yorker)

"A planet doesn't explode of itself," said drily
The Martian astronomer, gazing off into the air—
"That they were able to do it is proof that highly
Intelligent beings must have existed there."

IV

Quietly
He turned the key in the lock, and gave the good ship
To night and darkness and the oncoming stars.

What was this thing called "growing old"? All his life
He had heard about it, had read about it, had seen
Others grow old. He remembered his father's words:
"Someday, when I am gone and you are older,
Perhaps you will understand." 'Perhaps,' he had thought,
Wondering what really there was to understand
In that so improbable state. Dimly he sensed
That life, like an old legend told over and over,
To each of us throughout the generations
Is told for the first time, to each of us
Told once, once only, its tender passages
Of youth, of love, of joy, and that if you listened
Long enough, you would come to the part called "age,"
And after that came death. But never to him,
He would think—to others, but never to him, this incredible
Remote event! In the rush and hurly-burly
Of living, there was scant room for thoughts of death,
Much less of age, so that imperceptibly,
Almost as if in the winking of an eye,
The thing happened: waking from the long turmoil
And trance of youth, suddenly you found it there—
Not knowing what had become of the years between,
You found yourself, as now he found himself,
An agèd man pacing his father's acres,
Remembering how his father had said, "Someday,
When you are older, perhaps you will understand."
Was it not all exactly as foretold
Long since? Had it not happened all over again?
He had come to that passage in the old legend so many
Before him had listened to through the centuries—
But, oh, the difference, for now it was told to him,
And it wasn't believable! The tide of summer
Stood high in the land: the fragrance of honeysuckle,
Toward which the painted-lady and fritillary
Spread sunlit wings, mixed with the darker odors

Of earth and ocean; already an early cricket
Began his tentative tune; the humming-bird
Shook dew down from the flower of the trumpet-vine;
And in the woodland, where oven-bird and chat,
Flicker and wood-dove, thrush and vireo,
And an occasional phoebe, were the voices
Of this sea-drowsy country, the tiger-lily
Shone like a flame. These were his father's acres,
For so he still thought of them, though now they were his,
And dear and lovely as they ever had been,
Yes, dearer to him even than when in childhood
He and his brother had climbed the ancient oak,
Now fallen, that stood near the house, or when as a boy
He watched, at twilight, from some western window,
The young moon setting behind the sycamore,
While the evening-star brightened and the first bats
Circled the garden—yes, lovelier, dearer now
Almost to the point of heartbreak, for now the heart
Such memories haunted was stricken at every turn.
Things were no longer merely themselves, but all
Echoed one another in endless reverberations,
The past lived on in the present, something unearthly
Had entered the earth, and the swollen springs of feeling,
Long pent in the breast, were straining at overflow.
Now the thrush's song, heard in some earlier summer
With one well loved no longer here, could twist
The heart with an agony keener than any joy;
The familiar sound of the sea, forever shifting
Its weight of waters on far shores, awaken
Memories of that sound, heard long ago
In happier hours. He had come to that part of the legend
Time tells us if we live long enough to reach it,
And it is grave, for in that part of the legend
Those loved and no longer with us will outnumber
Those loved and with us still. He turned abruptly,

Retracing his steps along the path he had come,
Through woodlands of green light and gloom where the small
Wind-flowers flanked the way and, as he went,
Pondered his thoughts. Was it possible this stranger,
This agèd man pacing these woodland paths,
These well loved acres, was it possible this was he,
The youth who used to walk them? And by what devious
And hardly remembered passages of the past
Had he arrived here? He tried to call up that past,
Go back over those passages in the old legend
That Time was telling him, and rediscover
The way by which he had come. Vague memories
Welled up in him; old episodes, old scenes
From other days long vanished, came back to him;
Faces and forms of the belovèd dead
Appeared before him; like magic-lantern pictures
Cast on the screen of memory, they came
In marvellous procession: Harriet trimming
The Christmas tree; Ned, in their rooms at college,
Bent over some endless book; Sara's shy glance,
On parting; his father laughing at him; his mother
Listening to the new poem. How strange, how dim,
These images were! With all the strength he had,
With all his imagination, he strove to summon
Forth from these images the reality,
To bring before him again, in all their truth,
The darling men and women whose breathing presence
Still vibrated in the heart. But they remained
Beyond his summoning; these, who once had been
So near, so dear, had now become mere figures
In some old legend he had heard about—
And he believed in them as you believed
In the figures in an old legend. Oh, all those words,
Those cries, that life, that love, reaching out to us,
What did it mean, he thought, this show, this pageant

Paraded before the spirit! Was it not all
A monstrous allegory, whose forms and fictions
Were but the symbols of some secret thing
That Time was trying to tell us—we who, ourselves,
Were characters in the story? By now he had come
To the marble bench facing the lower garden,
And he rested there, sunk in his meditations.
The soliloquy of the sea, heard far away—
Sound without end; the excited, rain-sweet, fresh
Chatter of summer birds; slow pace and dazzle
Of summer clouds; the scent of flower and grass;
And the soft breath of summer on his cheek,
Mixed with his thoughts: the inner world and the outer
Interpenetrated and mingled; past and present,
As in the confusion of a waking dream,
Were blent in the one phantasmagoria,
Heightening each other; and more and more they came
Crowding, those echoes and images out of the years—
Faces, faces, of the living and the dead,
Laughing or grave, some tender, some grimacing
As if in mockery—endlessly they came,
A flood of memories stretching the taut spirit,
Too well aware how all would be soon withdrawn,
And straining to hold all. The long, sunlit hours
Found him still lost in reverie. Toward evening,
Like one awakened from a deep dream, he rose
And, leaving the garden by way of another path,
Mounted the slight incline to the old house.
The house he had once compared to "a great ship foundered
At the bottom of green sea-water" now seemed to him,
As it lay there lonely in the sad evening light,
More like a ship on some vast voyage bound
Into the unknown seas of space and time—
He thought of it as a vessel whose prow was plowing
The dark ocean of the stars, the immeasurable, shoreless

Waters of the future. What did that future hold,
He wondered now, for himself and for the world,
In the days to come? Where was the old ship steering,
Through a darkness such as had never before been known
In the long history of man? There was no foretelling.
There was none could say. But of one thing he was sure:
The fragile network of love that binds together
Spirit and spirit, over the whole earth,
Love—that by the very nature of things
Is doomed, is destined to heartbreak, mortal love,
Which is a form of suffering—here and now,
In its brief moment, yes even in its defeat,
Triumphs over the very nature of things,
And is the only answer, the only atonement,
Redeeming all. Far over, a waking star
Glimmered in the west of heaven. He opened the door,
And entered the house, the ship, where so many others
Had embarked as passengers, where one passenger now,
The dearest of all, awaited him. Quietly
He turned the key in the lock, and gave the good ship
To night and darkness and the oncoming stars.

(In memory of Van Wyck Brooks)

In the quiet before cockcrow when the cricket's
Mandolin falters, when the light of the past
Falling from the high stars yet haunts the earth
And the east quickens, I think of those I love—
Dear men and women no longer with us.

And not in grief or regret merely but rather
With a love that is almost joy I think of them,
Of whom I am part, as they of me, and through whom
I am made more wholly one with the pain and the glory,
The heartbreak at the heart of things.

I have learned it from them at last, who am now grown old
A happy man, that the nature of things is tragic
And meaningful beyond words, that to have lived
Even if once only, once and no more,
Will have been—oh, how truly—worth it.

The years go by: March flows into April,
The sycamore's delicate tracery puts on
Its tender green; April is August soon;
Autumn, and the raving of insect choirs,
The thud of apples in moonlit orchards;

Till winter brings the slant, windy light again
On shining Manhattan, her towering stone and glass;
And age deepens—oh, much is taken, but one
Dearer than all remains, and life is sweet
Still, to the now enlightened spirit.

Doors are opened that never before were opened,
New ways stand open, but quietly one door
Closes, the door to the future; there it is written,
"Thus far and no farther"—there, as at Eden's gate,
The angel with the fiery sword.

The Eden we dream of, the Eden that lies before us,
The unattainable dream, soon lies behind.
Eden is always yesterday or tomorrow,
There is no way now but back, back to the past—
The past has become paradise.

And there they dwell, those ineffable presences,
Safe beyond time, rescued from death and change.
Though all be taken, they only shall not be taken—
Immortal, unaging, unaltered, faithful yet
To that lost dream world they inhabit.

Truly, to me they now may come no more,
But I to them in reverie and remembrance
Still may return, in me they still live on;
In me they shall have their being, till we together
Darken in the great memory.

Dear eyes of delight, dear youthful tresses, foreheads
Furrowed with age, dear hands of love and care—
Lying awake at dawn, I remember them,
With a love that is almost joy I remember them:
Lost, and all mine, all mine, forever.

(*In memory of my father*)

Father, whom I knew well for forty years
Yet never knew, I have come to know you now—
In age, make good at last those old arrears.

Though time, that snows the hair and lines the brow,
Has equalled us, it was not time alone
That brought me to the knowledge I here avow.

Some profound divination of your own,
In all the natural effects you sought
Planted a secret that is now made known.

These woodland ways, with your heart's labor bought,
Trees that you nurtured, gardens that you planned,
Surround me here, mute symbols of your thought.

Your meaning beckons me on every hand,
Grave aisles and vistas, in their silence, speak
A language that I now can understand.

In all you did, as in yourself, unique—
Servant of beauty, whom I seek to know,
Discovering here the clue to what I seek.

When down the nave of your great elms I go
That soar their Gothic arches where the sky,
Nevertheless, with all its stars will show,

Or when the moon of summer, riding high,
Spills through the leaves her light from far away,
I feel we share the secret, you and I.

All these you loved and left. We may not stay
Long with the joy our hearts are set upon:
This is a thing that here you tried to say.

The night has fallen; the day's work is done;
Your groves, your lawns, the passion of this place,
Cry out your love of them—but you are gone.

O father, whom I may no more embrace
In childish fervor, but, standing far apart,
Look on your spirit rather than your face,

Time now has touched me also, and my heart
Has learned a sadness that yours earlier knew,
Who labored here, though with the greater art.

The truth is on me now that was with you:
How life is sweet, even its very pain,
The years how fleeting and the days how few.

Truly, your labors have not been in vain;
These woods, these walks, these gardens—everywhere
I look, the glories of your love remain.

Therefore, for you, now beyond praise or prayer,
Before the night falls that shall make us one,
In which neither of us will know or care,

This kiss, father, from him who was your son.

Yes, this is the place, and there is the great oak-tree
I climbed as a boy, on the drear dead branches now
A sinister evening-star stares downward fixedly.
          All shall be taken.

And here is the house: the gardens lie waste and bare;
The nymph of the fountain is fallen; in chamber and hall
No voices, no laughter; no footstep now upon floor, upon stair.
          All shall be taken.

And can *this* be the room where, oh, such aeons ago,
A young man grieved and exulted, can *this* have been me?
I need wonder no more what it's like to have died, who now
          stand here and know.
          All shall be taken.

How slowly we die, how many a well loved face
Time takes and, in taking, has taken a part of us too!
The stars have grown dimmer, the earth has become a less
          friendly place.
          All shall be taken.

Like swallows when summer is over, like the clear light
Of morning that fades into dusk, they vanish away,
And our autumn is on us, a gradual darkening, the first chill
          of night.
          All shall be taken.

Has the journey no end? Have I come already so far,
Trudging on, trudging on forever, only for this:
To stand in the country of age, under a fading star?
          All shall be taken.

Do we pass from nothing to nothing? Is the moment between
The only moment we have? Before it, is nothing.
After it, nothing. The moment itself will never have been.
          All shall be taken.

There is a mystery too deep for words;
The silence of the dead comes nearer to it,
Being wisest in the end. What word shall hold
The sorrow sitting at the heart of things,
The majesty and patience of the truth!
Silence will serve; it is an older tongue:
The empty room, the moonlight on the wall,
Speak for the unreturning traveller.

V

Glory of soundless heaven, wheel of stars
Round the bright axle-tree in silence turning!

Glory of soundless heaven, wheel of stars
Round the bright axle-tree in silence turning!
Trellis and cloudy vine! Great labyrinth
And wilderness of light! Hear, you proud flames
Hung high forever, your cold Medusa stare
Has turned a heart to stone.

Evening has quieted the wind, the night
Is soft around me while I sit alone,
And reading, by calm candle-light.

The voice of a forgotten poet cries,
From the clear page, up to my listening heart—
And my heart listens, and replies.

And yet, even in loveliness I find
No refuge from old wonder; the old thoughts
And the old questions come to mind.

Was it for this the ravin and the rage,
The lust and hunger of the centuries,
Clamored—to close in this calm page?

What blood was shed for this! What roving herds
In meadowy pastures, what brave things, have died
To feed the music of these words!

I will not think of this, I will read on
In these calm pages. It is written here:
The Song to the Belovèd One.

The heart that wrought it, and the cunning hand,
Are stilled forever, and the poet lies,
Forgotten, in a far-off land.

The iron bondage of old Time and Space
Withholds me from him, whom I have not seen—
Nor shall I look upon his face.

He takes his ease in the dark earth and there
Has rest from all his labors, and the night
Covers him with her heavy hair.

If I could pierce into that hushed abode
Of slumber and corruption, I should find
The mouth from which this sorrow flowed.

It would be quiet now, for all it cried—
Quiet and imperturbable: it is
With its own sleep preoccupied.

Yet, surely, in this very room it sings
Miraculously to my heart to-night!
How shall I understand these things?

I will not think of them, I will read on
In these calm pages. It is written here:
The Song to the Belovèd One.

The night is hushed around me while I move
Darkly, with dreaming thought, from page to page,
From line to line, of grief and love.

Now, in the silence of the night, I read
These words, the opening of the final prayer:
Song, for thy sake, with Death I plead.

The lonely splendor of Antares shines
Through the barred window, and an aphis crawls
Among the letters and the lines.

He moves among them with uncertain will,
Fitfully, and between the words, "I plead,"
Falters a moment—then is still.

Little he guesses what these letters are,
Nor I the meaning of the trembling Word
Written beyond us, star on star.

The night covers us both, and we are driven,
Like leaves before the wind, through the immense
And glittering wilderness of heaven.

Earth takes us with her; silently she swings
Through the old orbit, bearing in her breast
The drowsy mouth—the mouth that sings.

And yet, all this lives only in my mind,
And when that darkens, the whole world will darken
Suddenly—the whole world go blind.

All I have touched, all I have loved and known,
Will fail me—and the breast of life draw back,
Leaving me in the dark, alone.

O starry universe, hung in the clear
Vault of my mind, be living in me now—
Dwell in me for a moment here!

How often, in the many minds of men,
Have you been born, only to pass away—
Dying, with every mind, again!

This is a thought that is too hard for me:
It is a bitter thing to think upon,
That, to myself, all this shall be

As if it had not been—when I am gone.

Life, where your lone candle burns
In the darkness of the night,
Mothlike my lost spirit turns
Toward you, in its circling flight.

Steadily your beauty draws
Onward, with each hurrying breath—
Till I flutter, till I pause
In the radiance of death.

I am flaming, I am fled—
All around you reigns the night;
But my agony has fed
You, a moment, holy light.

We are all woven of the one weaving,
Flower and bird and beast and tree:
The gray kingfisher and the trout,
The toad that spreads a tiny hand
On the earth's carpet quietly—
Heaven, shaken with storm and thunder,
Clouds and great waters, winds and snows,
The starry firmament, the grieving
Heart of man; through earth and sea,
The moth, the tiger, and the rose,
Petal and planet—strand on strand—
The wandering threads wind in and out,
With warp and woof, over and under,
Weaving the ancient unity.

We are all woven in one story,
One legend like a sorrow runs
Through creeds and crowns and buried wars,
Prophets and saviours crucified,
Great fortresses, and cities, once
Crowded, now crumbled and forsaken,
Captains and kings of old that spread
Their sails upon the sea: one glory
Speaks through them all—through swords and guns,
Hopes and defeats, and hearts that bled,
Lovers, or rulers in their pride,
Desolate lands, and the lone stars
That by the wind of Time are shaken,
And thronging worlds and flaming suns.

We are all moving on together,
In mystery, to the end unknown—
Through all the ways and days of earth:
The thief, the ploughman and the seer,
The dog, the emperor on his throne,
The head, bowed over eyes unseeing,
The dying face, the broken heart,
To the one end are moving, whether
Evil or good—but not alone.
Each in the other has a part.
Each, as he may, in hope or fear,
Love, lust, or labor, death or birth,
Works out the will of the One Being—
For One is all, and all are One.

Night has its fear—
As the slow dusk advances, and the day
Fades out in fire along the starry way,
The ancient doubt draws near.

Vague shapes of dread,
Soft owl or moth, and timid, twittering things,
Move through the growing dark; on furtive wings
The bat flits overhead.

And in the house
The death-watch ticks; the dust of time is stirred
With timorous footfalls, in the night is heard
The gnawing of the mouse.

Through the old room
What phantoms throng, what ghosts that to and fro
Waver—and lips that laughed here long ago,
Long since gone to their doom!

A whip-poor-will
Bleakly across the baleful country cries
From a blurred mouth, and from the west replies
Echo—and all is still.

Now, from her cell,
Her body's prison, with the ancient doubt
And terror stricken, the scared soul looks out,
Asking if all be well.

Great kings have been,
Poets, and mighty prophets; shapes have cried
About the world, or moved in mournful pride,
And are no longer seen.

From many lands
Their plaint was lifted; from how many a shore
Sorrows have wailed, that are not any more!
They sleep, with folded hands.

They have their day:
Their cry is loud about the earth, who come
To the one end—the singing lips grow dumb
Always, in the one way.

Pondering these,
The fretful spirit, in bewilderment,
Quickens with a vague doubt, and, not content,
Broods—and is ill at ease.

Her being is
Throned on so frail a pulse, such fleeting breath
Bears up her dream across the gulf of death
And the obscure abyss.

Always she hears
The hurtling chariots of the hurrying blood,
Her shuttling breath that in the solitude
Weaves the one self she wears.

Now first the sheer
Veil over heaven dissolves, and bares the whole
Shining reality, which in the soul
Wakens an ancient fear.

Darkness reveals
The tragic truth: her will sinks hopeless wings
Before the inexorable fact of things,
Humbling the dread she feels.

With the old awes
Confronted, and the flaming mystery,
She may not speak—but, pondering, suddenly
Grows silent, and withdraws.

Her thoughts ascend,
Star beyond star, height beyond aching height
Upward, in adoration infinite,
Forever, without end.

Here in my curving hands I cup
This quiet dust. I lift it up.

Here is the mother of all thought,
Of this the shining heavens are wrought,
The laughing lips, the feet that rove,
The face, the body that you love:
Mere dust, no more—yet nothing less;
And this has suffered consciousness,
Passion and terror; this again
Shall suffer passion, death, and pain.

For, as all flesh must die, so all,
Now dust, shall live. 'Tis natural,
Yet hardly do I understand—
Here in the hollow of my hand
A bit of God Himself I keep,
Between two vigils fallen asleep.

Move with a dancing step to a sad music

In agonizing dance,
With fierce reluctant love,
To the measure of that song
In which they live and move,
In iron governance
All things are whirled along.
All things that live and are,
Breathless or drawing breath,
Atom and man and star,
Time's cycle and renewal,
Rhythms of birth and death,
Are dancing to that song,
Inflexible and cruel,
By the one music bound
Whose counterpoint is pain.
As the great song turns round
They turn, retreat, advance,
Follow the pattern through,
Retreat, advance again,
Longingly, loathingly,
As the music bids them do—
And all dance, dance,
In that great agony.

All living things, all flesh,
Earth's violent wills at war,
Striving with one another,
Dying, each of the other,
In the bloody web of things
Tangled, the carnal mesh,
In toils of the struggle bound
That each was fashioned for—
In lust and agony
Woven of one another

In the brute clash of things—
As the great song wheels round,
(The primal dissonance),
They tread the harsh measure through,
Do as they have to do;
And all dance, dance,
In that great agony.

The atom, a whirling storm,
Hushed fury of force
Locked on itself, the swarm
Of the stars in heaven, too,
Locked each in its course,
Straining against the tether,
By the one music bound,
To the one truth held true
That holds all things together
In iron bondage held
As the great song comes round;
In agony compelled,
Out of that agony
"God! God!" they cry,
"Joy! Joy!" they cry—
Oh, the joy is agony,
That agony is joy—
"Dance, dance," they cry,
"Dance, dance for joy,
In the great agony!"

Man, in his journey through the centuries,
Now finds himself in that dark wood
Where, as Dante says, the right way is lost.
Oh, words that foretell all our perplexities—
Man, half angel and half ape,
Who, in his long ascension and escape
From the bestial, has withstood
Such toils, such perils, and subdued
To himself all other creatures, has not crossed
More than halfway the bridge whose span
Measures the abyss between the human and the brute—
The human that is yet to be—Man,
Who has weighed the stars in their solitudes; set foot
On the moon's surface; or with hateful war
Darkened the planet; dissected flower and root
And all created things, even to the core
Of the atom; and caused to be
Audible here that which since time began
Had sounded always in eternity,
The music of a Bach; or hurled
Into the dark new stars that take their place
In the firmament of night; whose face
Is turned skyward, whose eyes scan
Heaven for still another world,
Another planet for his conquest—Man,
Half angel and half ape,
Surely, he enters now that dark wood
Where, as Dante tells us, the right way is lost,
From which, as Dante discovered, there is no escape
Save by descent into hell and purgatory,
And thence, if so may be,
Out of the torments of fire and ice,
All perils passed,
Guided by love at last,
Up the long steep ascent to paradise.

Leave starry heaven behind,
Enter the atom, shrink
Into the vast, and find
You stand upon the brink
Of starry heaven again—
There where you were you are,
Full circle come again
On a journey circular,
Through the atom back to the stars.

We live in a world that, for the most part,
Doesn't know us. We move as strangers
Among rocks, trees, rivers, mountains,
Unaware that we are here; even the house
We dwell in and are fond of, perhaps,
Has no knowledge of our existence; the rose
Can't tell our touch from the touch of the wind,
And a thousand stars look out and do not see us.
As for other creatures, to most of them,
Except the domesticated ones, of course,
Who regard us, if at all, as magicians
Capable of the best and the worst, we occur
Chiefly as accidents, often unpleasant—
They have excommunicated us
From their society, who are crueller
Even than themselves, they are no longer
On speaking terms with us, we can't
Come very close to any wild thing;
The wren that builds in the eaves of our dwelling
Knows of us only as probable menace,
As possible beneficence; and the ant,
Whose counties we take in our stride, and whose townships
We level with a step, has never heard of us,
Or, if he has, it is no more
Than our own dim sense of the unknown beings
Who bestride us here, as we the ant,
Or move among us invisible
And merciful as the best of us sometimes are
When we sidestep the anthill, ruthless
As the best of us sometimes have to be when the tragic
Nature of things makes it necessary.
There is something wistful in our attitude
Toward things—the beautiful indifference
Of mountains or of a flower. The conscious

Desires, and is envious of,
The unconscious: man envies the rock
Its strength, its self-sufficient calm
Outwardly at least, though it represents
The locked fury of billions of atoms—
He moves, lonely and a stranger, among
The things that surround him, with which to fall in love
Is like courting a woman who is asleep.
Oh, almost everything seems to be asleep,
And cannot respond: the rose will not answer,
Nor the earth reply to her lover, the moon
Is unmindful of the poet who addresses her.
Head over heels in love, we dwell
Among beautiful things, like outcasts,
Even while they abide in us,
Who have won them into ourselves and by a supreme
Act of love and faith given them
Another dimension, engendering on them,
Through the embrace of matter by spirit,
The divine reality born of this fusion,
So that they become other than they were:
The moon that shines in your consciousness
Is more than mere mass and luminous contour,
And the rhythm of the surf along the shore
More than mere water in motion, something
Important has been created through the embrace
Of matter by spirit. But, oh, how cold,
How indifferent, is the response of that partner
To our burning love! I have sometimes thought
That the steady immersion of matter in spirit,
Throughout the ages, its being dipped
Again and again in the quivering, fleeting
Film of consciousness that overlies
The turning planet must, in time,
So saturate matter as to infect it

With spirit itself, and thus evoke,
In flower and tree, in wind and water,
The response for which we long; I have thought
That the brilliant sphere that out of dark heaven
Stares into a human mind
Might almost in that mirror discover
Itself, in wonder, there—a star,
Become so at last through fusion with spirit,
Which, by a depth of love that is
Adoring perception, fulfills an otherwise
Unfulfilled Creation. Nevertheless,
We have not roused nature from that sleep of hers—
Things remain things, we remain
Their lovers still, and wistfully
Dwell among them, who deeply abide in us,
Yet are ignorant of our presence here,
And will not know it when we are gone.

I live in an old house on a dark star
In the wilderness of heaven. Through these rooms,
Where I so many a time have seen them pass,
Men and women, some of them my own blood,
Still move in memory—their absence here
Is like an echo, the whip-poor-will at twilight
Laments them and the little owls cry out
Their legendary names, whom I have cherished.
It is hard to understand. At night the sea,
That moves upon the bare bed of this star,
Turns in her sleep and tells me marvellous things,
How there is no beginning and no end
But all flows on forever. And other stars
Look out at me, the intolerable glory of heaven,
To which the ages have lifted hands in vain,
Stares down upon me from a thousand eyes
Its shining secret. Here upon my shelf,
In half-forgotten volumes, old and worn,
Spirits out of the past that once were men
And walked the earth, now shrunken to the measure
Of a head-hunter's trophy, row on row,
Like birds in covered cages, bide their time
To do my will when I shall bid them speak.

Sacred is the communion of man with man
Through speech; dearer than wine, dearer than bread,
Is the low talk around the open fire
Or under the clear stars, whereby his heart
Is mingled with the heart of his own kind.
After the fret and turmoil of the day,
The tired seamstress leans into the twilight,
And, in the alley, with her neighbor shares
Grave gossip; while in billiard-room or bar,
To thunder of laughter, the old joke goes round,
Or ribald story. Wherever two are met,
There speech is, and the ancient fellowship,
Making us one, who are but wanderers
Upon a lonely way.

             And therefore men,
That death itself may not divide them forever,
Have shared with one another across the years,
In rune or rhyme, ballad, fable or myth,
Their passions and their sorrows—and a glory
Gathers about his memory who most
Has shared with us, out of his love, himself.
Blessèd beyond all others are the heads
Upon whose front falls the immortal gleam—
In distant lands perhaps, beyond far seas,
From sun-washed islands or gray promontories,
Lifted across the years to give us light—
Spirits at which our groping youth was fed,
The drowsy lips from which all dreams come down,
Makers of music, whisperers of secrets,
Though in the darkness of the centuries
Hidden away—the hands folded, the heart
Quiet—still musical, still murmuring
(In many a legend, many a rustling page,
Sad songs and dreams that drift about the world)

The old incorrigible ecstasy—
Despite all death, despite all doubt, all doom,
Still passionate, still intimate with us,
And full of a fierce love.

And good it is
To sit—echoing spirit and singing spirit—
As friend with friend, by the wayside of the years,
Above the dust of time and circumstance,
And hear, in the lone hour of delight,
The sacred things that man has said to man
For solace of his sad and wondering heart,
News from a traveller on the common way—
How the land lies, whether the hills be steep
Or valleys fruitful, where the waters run,
Or March hides the first flower—ponderings,
Praise of the road, doubt for the journey's end
Or of the purpose of the pilgrimage,
(If there *be* purpose in the pilgrimage),
Questions, questions, and reassurances,
Words that the generations past have worn
Upon their lips, for love's sake—that shall lie,
Trembling, upon the lips we may not reach:
The immortal Legend, the old tameless Song,
Wherein, to us—who all too easily,
Too often and too easily, forget—
The splendor, the unimaginable splendor,
Holy and stern, of all reality,
In happy moments is revealed anew;
Hints of a meaning, echoes of the high
Sorrowful music to which all things move,
With all their warring voices, to one end,
Violently. Amen—so *shall* they move,
Till Time's lone harp fall silent, till the years
Slumber, and all be as a tale long told.

Over the meadow-land
Where I so often have watched them,
To an ancient sound of the sea
Heavy upon this coast,
The summer stars look down—
A part of them, yet separate,
Singled by consciousness,
I stand and survey them here.
Deneb, Vega, Altair,
Hang high in the pure vault,
Trembling, and far below them
Venus, a fiery bloom
Fallen from the bough of heaven,
The great galactic vine,
Is glowing deep in the west.
Now from the fields unnumbered
Small creatures lift their hymn,
Cricket and grasshopper
Welcome with shrill noise
The illustrious presences,
They are here, they are here, they are here,
The glory that dwells in darkness
Has visited earth once more.
The heavens preserve their secret,
From the rim of the huge vault
To the high sidereal arches
No sound. Perpetual silence!
Infinite peace! But oh,
Universe of hushed light,
That peace will not deceive me;
Horrible process, divine
Agony and splendor,
Too well I know your ways,
Their grandeur and their vileness:
The tenderness, the brute

Bestiality, the bloody
Pattern of things on earth,
The fangs that rend the living
Body, the cruel delight,
The terror and the torment,
I know them—and in the heavens
Your dread and violent way
From nebula to system,
The throes of your vast elation,
Convulsions, whirlwinds of stars,
Fierce galaxies without number,
Staining the virgin darkness.
Also, the high sublime
Way of your lonely dreaming
In arches of ordered color
Where the rainbow curves the light
Over a trailing cloud,
The sorrow of void sea-spaces,
And the bolt of bright flame,
And the listening heart of a mother—
I know them, O divine truth,
Who stand here, for a moment
Permitted while the red blood
In leaping faithfulness flushes
Body and brain with the old
Incomparable elixir—
Permitted so, for a time,
To be aware of you now,
To worship and to adore you,
Holy substance of things,
From which the body of love
Is fashioned, the oceanic
Rhythm, the wild spring rain,
And the music of a Beethoven,
And of which I too am part

Forever. Oh, consoling
Thought, forever, forever
One with your timeless being,
More fully even than now,
When the temporal separation
Through consciousness shall be ended,
That consciousness in which
So briefly you were mirrored;
O sole and perfect truth,
When I lie down to mix
With your beauty in the darkness,
When I drag your glory down,
With me, into the grave.

Always the heavy air,
The dreadful cage, the low
Murmur of voices, where
Some force goes to and fro
In an immense despair.

As through a haunted brain—
With tireless footfalls
The obsession moves again,
Trying the floor, the walls,
Forever, but in vain.

In vain, proud force! A might,
Shrewder than yours, did spin
Around your rage that bright
Prison of steel, wherein
You pace for my delight.

And oh, my heart, what doom,
What warier will, has wrought
The cage, within whose room
Paces your burning thought,
For the delight of Whom?

He is an eye that watches in secret, an ear that would
Listen for what can only be overheard,
A mouth to tell us something we have forgotten—in a word,
To tell us all over again
Something we always knew. Oh, if he only could!

This is his torment and supreme
Challenge: for words are clumsy symbols, inadequate,
And reality is subtle and very great—
Greater by far than we have guessed
Is everyday reality, stranger than any dream.

Deep in him always the intuition is there
That something more than what is seen and heard is meant,
Something lost with the innocent
Delight and wonder that habit will destroy,
And which to recapture is his prime despair.

Slant moonlight on a meadow of cocked hay
Toward dawn, or sunlight falling through still apple trees,
What nudges him here, what speaks from these?
The silence of the stars or of the dead,
What is it trying to say?

The cacaphonic roar
Where Broadway and Forty-second meet,
The sombre flow of bodies through avenue and street—
These are things will bear much thinking about,
They are what they seem and something more.

Oh, to discover the formula, the device,
That will give us back forgotten reality again,
So we may share it with others then—
By the flow of a line, the fall of a word, to re-open a door,
If but for an instant, into lost paradise!

Such is the constant dream that keeps him strong
Through days of labor, sleepless nights,
Strange miseries and delights—
It is the cause of many a wound he takes,
The perpetual hope behind his song.

Living, he may be widely heard and become well known,
Or his fame wait upon days that are yet to be.
Dead, the branch he clung to on life's tree
Will tremble a little, for a little while,
Like a branch from which some bird, a nightingale perhaps,
    has flown.

Father, in a benign hour,
In the bare solitude of the beaches,
By the naked solitude of the sea,
In the immense solitude of heaven,
You uncovered your face,
And I worshipped you.

In the strict simplicity of light,
To the sound of the sea's thunder,
In the silence of your light,
My music fell from me
Like a forgotten tune.

O all-beholding father,
You who have looked upon the Pharaohs,
And upon the Crucifixion on Golgotha
And the passing generations of mankind,
There came no cloud between us,
Creator and creature were one,
In the bare solitude of the beaches,
By the naked solitude of the sea,
In a benign hour,
In the silence of your light.

That glimmering window-pane,
Toward morning, is the whisper of a star,
The god who created, whose energies sustain,
The worlds around him, and all that on them are.
That glimmering window-pane
Is a message from the god, and seems to say,
"Darkness and night are past,
I bring you a new day,
Not yet your last."

INDEX OF FIRST LINES

ABOUT THE AUTHOR

John Hall Wheelock was born on Long Island and educated at Harvard and in Germany. His first published poem appeared in 1900 in the Morristown, New Jersey, school paper.

Mr. Wheelock is the author of ten books of poetry and of one prose work, *What Is Poetry?* During his distinguished career as a poet he has received numerous awards, among them the Bollingen Prize in Poetry, and the Signet Society Medal for Distinguished Achievement in the Arts. He is a member of The American Academy of Arts and Letters, a Chancellor of The Academy of American Poets, and an Honorary Consultant in American Letters to The Library of Congress.

Mr. Wheelock continues to publish frequently, and new poems of his have recently appeared in *The Sewanee Review* and *The New Yorker*.